THE COMPOST HEAP

by Harlow Rockwell

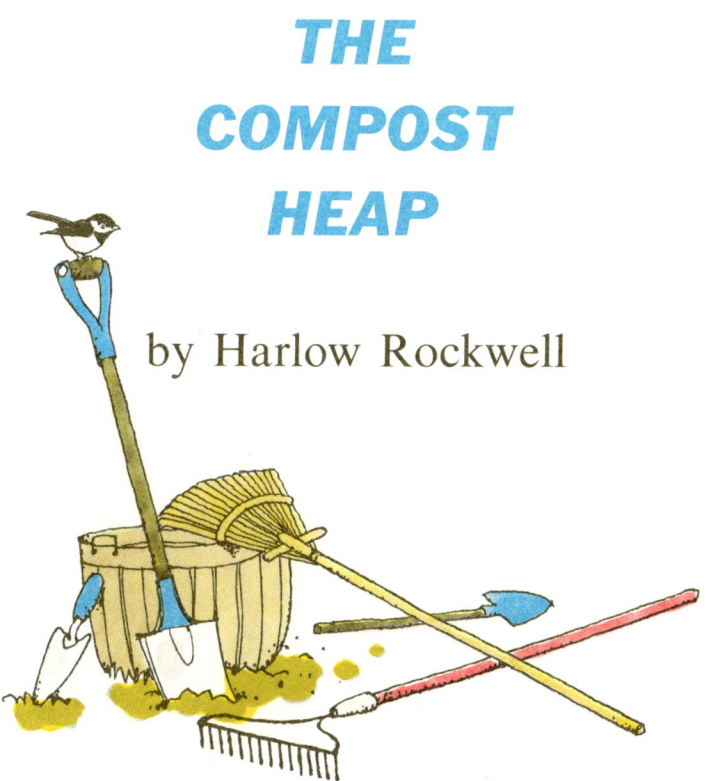

DOUBLEDAY & COMPANY, INC. GARDEN CITY, NEW YORK

Library of Congress Cataloging in Publication Data
Rockwell, Harlow.
  The compost heap.

  SUMMARY: Explains simply how a compost heap is made
and how it turns into soil.

  1. Compost—Juvenile literature. [1. Compost.
2. Soil] I. Title.
S661.R57   631.8'75
ISBN 0-385-06822-0
ISBN 0-385-08989-9 (lib. bdg.)
Library of Congress Catalog Card Number 73-10544

Copyright © 1974 by Harlow Rockwell
All Rights Reserved
Printed in the United States of America
First Edition

for
Hannah, Lizzy
& Olly

My father dug a hole in the ground
and filled it with last fall's
raked-up leaves.

He called it a compost heap.
There was a pit in the center

to hold the rain
and keep the leaves wet.

Snow covered the compost heap until spring came.

The leaves were wet and brown and slippery and they smelled like a forest.

We put green weeds

and grass cuttings on the compost heap.

Coffee grounds and tea leaves,
orange peel and apple parings,
an old potato and some onion skin,

a banana peel, watermelon rinds and seeds
and some broken eggshells—

all went on the compost heap.

Summer rains fell
and the warm sun shone

and the weeds sprouted and the eye
of the old potato grew into a green plant.

Worms wriggled

in the compost heap when my father
and I turned it over with our rakes.
It steamed.

Things rotted.

Things sprouted.

I never saw so many worms.

And the compost heap turned to earth.
We put it in a bushel basket

and spread it on

our garden.

NAPPANEE PUBLIC LIBRARY
N.   , INDIANA

98744